Bead Jewelry & Wire Wrapping for Beginners

A Complete Timeless Guide of How to Create Binding Pieces of Jewelry

(Including The Top Easy To Follow Projects to Get You Started)

Introduction

Have you ever looked at a certain piece of jewelry and wondered, "how was this gorgeous piece of jewelry made?"

If you have, this guide shall introduce you to the art of bead jewelry and wire wrapping so that you can create binding pieces of jewelry.

In it, you will learn:

- What bead jewelry and wire wrapping entails

- **The tools and supplies you need for the job**

- The types of wires that are best suited for the job and how to choose the best wire for your project

- **How to get started – where to begin**

- How to create basic wire links

- **Simple projects to get you started**

- And much more

What's more; the book takes a beginner friendly, step by step approach to break down seemingly complex concepts into easy to follow steps that you can follow.

Bead Jewelry

So even if you are a complete beginner, you will find the book immensely helpful and easy to follow.

Let's begin.

Bead Jewelry

Table of Content

Introduction 2

Table of Content 4

Chapter 1: Introduction to Wire Wrapping 6

   History Of Wire Wrapping _____ 7

Chapter 2: Tools and Supplies Used In Wire Wrapping _____ 8

Chapter 3: Types Of Wire _____ 18

   Dead Soft vs. Half Hard Wire _____ 22

   Wire Shapes _____ 24

Chapter 4: Getting Started With Wire Wrapping _____ 27

Chapter 5: How to Create Basic Wire Links 30

Chapter 6: How to Make Simple Wire-Wrapped Pendants _____ 35

Chapter 7: How to Make a Basic 2-Wire Weave _____ 43

Chapter 8: Sword Pendant Wire Wrapped Jewelry _____ 48

Chapter 9: Wrapped Stacked Wire Ring__ 58

Chapter 10: Old Fashioned Chain Wire __ 64

Chapter 11: Turtle Bracelet _____ 69

Chapter 12: Figure 8 Chain _____ 72

Chapter 13: Grape Cluster Earrings _____ 77

Step 14: Fabric Wrapped Choker Necklace 82

Chapter 15: DIY Anthropology Perched Harmonies Necklace _____ 88

Conclusion _____ 92

Chapter 1: Introduction to Wire Wrapping

Wire wrapping is probably among the oldest methods of creating handmade jewelry. The technique uses jewelry wire and wire-like things —such as headpins—to make jewelry components. The jeweler then connects individual wire components using mechanical techniques with no heating or soldering.

Wire wrapping involves tasking a wire and wrapping it around itself, beads, or any other components to make jewelry. You can use this technique to create a loop for joining different components, such as when wrapping a pendant or creating a wrapped wire loop.

Through wire wrapping, you can also secure beads to a form or attach non-bead items —for instance, wire wrapping rhinestone cup chain— onto a bangle. The wire itself can act as a design detail or become the structure and foundation of your piece when wrapped, manipulated, curved, and bent.

Wire wrapping allows you to create custom shapes and angles and thus offers you more ways to use different components together. The technique of wrapping the wire around itself gives this craft its name —wire wrapping

History Of Wire Wrapping

Examples of wire and beaded jewelry created through wire wrapping techniques date back to thousands of years.

The British Museum acquired samples of jewelry having spiraled wire components from the Sumerian Dynasty found in The Royal Cemetery at U. This sort of jewelry dates back to 2000 BC, approximately.

Other jewelry discovered in Ancient Rome depicts wire wrapped loops, which is one of the techniques used in making wire wrapped jewelry. Such Roman jewelry dates back to 2000 years ago, approximately.

Further on in history, wire wrapping techniques especially improved after the development of soldiering because it was a quick and economical way to create jewelry components out of wire.

Wire wrapping techniques are not popularly used for jewelry that is mass-produced given that machines can mold (cast) jewelry components a lot faster, more precisely, and cheaply. Individual jewelers are primarily the ones who employ the wire wrapping approach to jewelry making.

Chapter 2: Tools and Supplies Used In Wire Wrapping

When you're just getting started with wire wrapping, you don't have to spend a lot of money on tools, especially if you don't think you'll be using the tools frequently.

Just keep in mind that substandard tools may not be as comfortable to hold; they also tend to wear out quicker. If you think you'll be using your tools frequently, its best to have good tools.

Below are the few tools and supplies you need to get started with wire wrapping:

#1: Wire

The first thing you need to acquire for wire wrapping is the wire itself. You wouldn't have anything to wrap minus the wire.

Bead Jewelry

As a beginner, you should use copper wire because it's easier to work with and much cheaper. Later on, once you are ready to begin marketing your designs, you can use sterling silver wire.

#2: Pliers

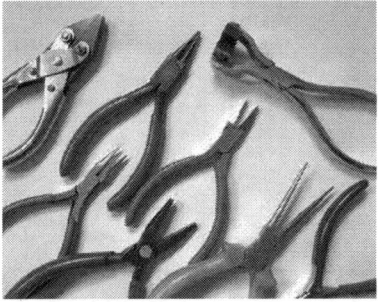

You may have as many pliers as you want for wrapping. However, to get started, you need some chain nose pliers and round nose pliers.

#3: Cutters

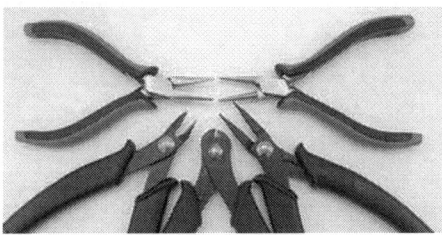

the wire flush will require to be cut and a pair of scissors or a knife is not going to cut it.

#4: Mallets and hammers

You will at least need a rawhide mallet for strengthening the wire at the base frame.

#5: Ruler

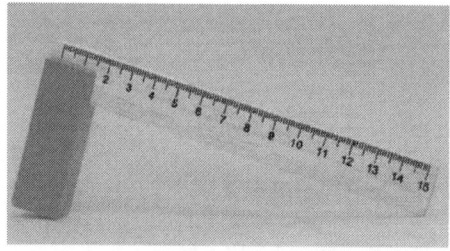

You will need a ruler for measuring the wire you require for cutting your pieces.

#6: Sharpie pen

You will need a sharpie pen or something similar for marking the wire that you will be using for bending or cutting.

#7: Ring mandrel

This tool is absolutely necessary for making rings.

#8: Bracelet mandrel

Bead Jewelry

This is a tool you need if you intend to make bracelets. You should get the oval one, but the round one works as well.

#9: Sandpaper or files

You will need these supplies for smoothing out the pointy ends of wire that is cut.

#10: Round nose pliers

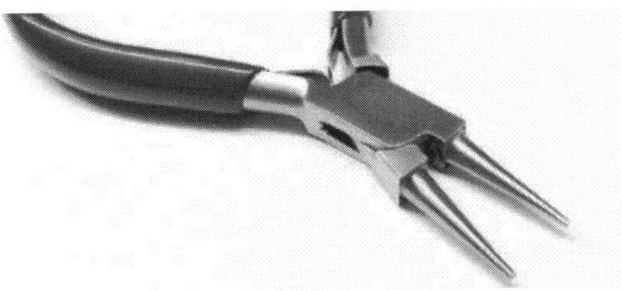

These pliers comprises of cone-shaped jaws that are tapered. They are used for making curves and creating loops in wire.

The round nose pliers are imperative for basic and advanced wire wrapping techniques such as making eye pins, wrapped loops, ear wires, rosary chains, and wrapping briolettes and headpins to create dangles and other designs. Make sure you select round nose pliers which fit in your hand comfortably to avoid wrist and hand pain from use over a long period.

Select a pair that has longer handles if you have large hands and the other way round for smaller hands. You should also consider acquiring pliers with handles that are soft cushioned instead of plastic or hard rubber handles. Others also consider looking for ones with a lengthy jaw which is very fine at the end so that you may enjoy more distinctions in the loop sizes you can create with just this single tool.

#11: Chain nose pliers

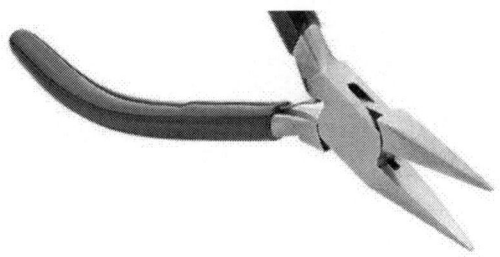

They have ends that are tapered, smooth and flat on the edges inside. You mustn't use pliers that have ridges as they are going to leave behind visible impressions on your wire and damage it while you work.

These pliers are essential for the basic techniques of jewelry making such as straightening kinks in wire, tucking in wrapped wire ends, flattening crimp beads, closing and opening jump rings, bending wire, and many more. You should never use these pliers to create loops.

Select a pair that fits your hands comfortably —like the round nose pliers. Consider how long the handles are and the material used to make the handles. You can also select a pair that's fine at the end so that you may use them in spaces that are tight– such as when you tuck in the tips of the wire after you complete a loop that is wire wrapped.

#12: Flush cutters

This is a tool for wire cutting that will leave the tip of the wire that has been cut nearly faultlessly flat. This is unique about this tool because other cutters don't permit you to get up close to your project to cut precisely where you want to cut and they often result in a 'bur' on the tip of your wire on either sides of the cut. Using these cutters reduces the steps needed to get clean ends on the beaded jewelry and nicely finished wire wraps.

When selecting flush cutters, choose one with a tip that's finely pointed so that after the wrapping, you may be able to clip immediately following the wire.

NOTE

If you are using memory wires, don't use flush cutters as doing this will destroy the cutter. Also, try preserving your flush cutters' fine ends of by only using them to clip the wire in compact spaces only. For dissimilar cuts, try using the back or middle of your cutter jaw.

Flush Cutters vs. Regular Wire Cutters

What's the difference between flush cutters and regular wire cutters?

For starters, the conventional wire cutters tend to be clunky, something that makes them not suitable for use in fine wire work. On the other hand, the flush cutters have smaller, pointed tips that are more suitable for creating precision cuts in tight areas.

As earlier mentioned, regular wire cutters leave a bur on either side of the wire, that is different from cuts made by flush cutters. Cutting with the flush cutters leaves a flat cut one side of the wire, which is optimal in most jewelry making techniques.

Chapter 3: Types Of Wire

When it comes to jewelry making through wire wrapping, there are a variety of choices regarding the kind of metals you can use to make your jewelry, including base metal wires and precious metal wires.

These options include plated wire, filled (overlay) wire, anodized wire, enamel-coated colored wire, and solid metal wire.

#: Solid Precious Metal wire

This type of wire is the best option for high-end craft designs and jewelry. Choices in this category include Argentium® sterling silver, 925 sterling silver, and 999 fine silver wire. Argentium is an alloy that is tarnish-resistant — meaning that both you and the end-user will consume less time polishing.

#: Silver Fill & Gold fill wire

Also referred to as overlay, the creation of these types of wires uses pressure and heat to layer a thick lay of precious metal onto a base of a less expensive metal.

When making high-end designer jewelry, but you require something more thrifty as compared to solid precious metal wire, the silver fill and gold fill wires are the best option. In spite of not being solid, we consider overlay/fill a precious metal since the surface of the precious metal is significantly thicker than a metal plating.

Solid Base Metal wire

This type of wire works well for creating finished artisan jewelry. It is also commonly used as a practice-material for making models for precious metal designs. You will find copper wire at the top of the list here.

Other choices include bronze, brass, nickel silver (also called German silver), and stainless steel. The base metal that you select will highly depend on the color of your intended design; however, learning about the characteristics of different metals might also aid you in choosing.

Silver-plated and Gold-plated wire

This type of plated wire will yield colors matching the components of the precious metal minus the extra cost. The limitation of silver or gold plated wire is that the plating can crack and eventually chip to reveal the base metal underneath if you over-manipulate the wire. Consequentially, a wire that is plated is ideal for jewelry designs that don't need extensive wrapping and bending.

Enamel coated wire

This type of wire provides a variety of permanent colors that won't crack or chip. One of the topmost brands is Artistic Wire®, which is created from copper wire that is covered with a permanently colored enamel coating.

For colors that are silver-plated, you will find a pure silver layer in between the last permanent enamel layer and the copper wire. That gives the silver-plated colors a brilliant, rich shine.

We consider Artistic wire 'dead soft.' Ensure that you are careful enough to avoid scraping through the layer that is colored even if the finish won't crack or chip. Most wire workers either coat the tip of their tool with Tool Magic® or they use nylon jaw pliers.

Anodized wire

This wire provides a variety of bright colors which are made in a chemical bath. The colors are longer lasting as compared to the plated ones since these colors are non-plated. You need to be careful when working with this type of wire, to avoid scraping through it. Like the enamel-coated wire, most wire workers simply coat the tips of their tools with Tool Magic® or use nylon jaw pliers.

Memory wire

This type of wire provides a couple of sizes of wire coils that maintain their oval or round shape – similar to the old springy Slinky toy. The wire is perfect for making multistrand bracelets, beaded wine charms, chokers, and rings. Ideally, Flat memory wire is excellent as a foundation for beads lashing.

Bullion (also called French wire)

The bullion wire is a delicate wire that is tightly coiled. This wire is used to protect and cover the final loops of the bead cord on bracelets and necklaces. It is available in extra-heavy, heavy, medium, and fine. You can choose from base metal and sterling silver options.

Dead Soft vs. Half Hard Wire

Sometimes when picking the type of wire to work with, you get the choice of selecting "half hard" or "dead soft" wire.

As suggested by the name, Dead soft wire is very easy to bend; you can even bend it using your hands. The benefit of dead soft wire is that it is easy to shape. Half hard wire, on the other hand, offers some resistance when you attempt to bend it. The benefit of half hard wire is that it maintains its shape better once it has been shaped.

The more you use a piece of wire, the more it hardens naturally; we refer to this as work hardening the wire. It is possible to hammer the wire to harden it once you have accomplished the shape you desire.

Using a nylon or rawhide hammer with care can harden the wire without altering the shape, use of a chasing hammer can flatten it nicely, and using a ball-peen hammer will give the wire a dappled texture.

Whether you purchase dead soft or half hard is usually just a matter of personal preference. Nonetheless, below are some general guidelines to aid you in getting started:

- Half hard is nice for creating jewelry components that require to hold their shape – bracelet forms, necklace foundations, jump rings, clasps, ear wires, etc.

- Dead soft wire works well when making flowing curves and spirals

- Generally, Silver fill and gold fill wire are harder in comparison to dead soft fine silver or sterling silver wire and are usually nearer to half hard

- Dead soft is the wire most used for wire wrapping and wire weaving including "sculpted" wire jewelry and wrapped cabochons

- Half hard creates distinct, sharp angles

When you are uncertain about which type of wire to use, pick dead soft wire. As mentioned, the wire becomes stiffer and brittler the more you use it — work hardening.

If you happen to purchase a wire that's too malleable for what you intend to do, you can try hardening it yourself using a tumbler, a draw plate, a wire whacker, or a nylon-head hammer. When your wire becomes too stiff for what you intend to do, re-soften it by annealing it —heating then allowing it cool gradually.

You can find jewelry wire in shapes such as half-round, square, round, and patterns such as pre-twisted and flat, all of which we shall discuss below. Jewelry wire is also available in a wide range of materials.

Brass and copper wire are easy to manipulate and shape. Wire made of brass is a little more rigid than copper, but it can be quite easy to manipulate. Wire made of Copper is easy to hammer until quite thin. Wire made of Sterling silver is soft enough to manipulate; however, once it has formed, it holds its shape well.

You make gold-filled wire by fusing a layer of 12 or 14 karat gold to a supporting material —that's the process used to make wire that is wire silver filled. The bond formed between the two materials is permanent.

Wire Shapes

The shape of the wire is what you see when you look at a cross-section of it, the cut end. Here're the different kinds of wire shapes:

Round

Round is the most common shape and is the standard shape used in most wire working.

Square

As the nooks of square wire offer a distinct physical appearance to completed jewelry, the use of square-shaped wire is usually just for aesthetic reasons. If you need to put a few wire flush pieces against one another, the square wire also offers a practical advantage. The square wire has flat sides that can lay flush in a manner that the round wire cannot. This is what makes the square wire very popular in designs for banding. In addition, for a sparkling effect, you can try twisting square wire using a pin vise.

Half round

This type of wire shape finds common use as a way to join various square wire pieces that are adjacent. The square wires are placed against the half round wire's flat side to leave the round side revealed in the completed design — banding.

Twisted (or fancy)

This type of shape provides aesthetic and textural qualities to wirework. The 'fancy' shape can be in the form of square or round wires.

You can make twisted wire with a Beadalon® wire twister or pin vise —you may also just purchase ready-made twisted wire. When you do decide to make twisted wire, remember that the gauge of the finished wire is going to be thicker than the single wires you have at the start of designing the piece.

We measure wire by diameter, which is pointed out by gauge numbers. The lower the gauge you use, the thicker your wire will be.

A 12 or 14 gauge wire is somewhat heavy but ideal for making chokers and bangles. A 10 gauge wire is stiff and very thick while a 26 gauge wire is fine-threaded, almost as thin as hair —this thin wire is excellent for coiling embellishments. The 16 gauge wire is suitable for making jump rings and links for bracelets and necklaces. The 18 gauge wire is great to use for making finer links and adding embellishments.

Chapter 4: Getting Started With Wire Wrapping

To get started with wire wrapping:

Supplies

Having the right supplies is one of the crucial parts about making jewelry. For operating and making jewelry, you are going to need wire cutters, curved nose pliers, round nose pliers, needle nose pliers, and, obviously, the wire.

Looping

Making the loops is the most essential and the first wire wrapping jewelry technique you will need to learn. As much as this is the most straightforward part of jewelry making, it is also the foundation of all the other designs that involve the use of wire that you could ever desire to make.

You will want to hold the wire in using the round nose pliers when making your loop. Using your fingers, begin to push the wire away from you. The loops, however, can also help you make space in between the beads.

Beads

The use of some techniques for wire wrapping can add some real grace to the beaded jewelry. To incorporate beads to the wire jewelry, begin by sliding the bead to the wire. Grasp the wire using a suitable flat nose pliers once the bead is securely on the wire, and then fold the wire at a right angle from you using your finger.

If however you want to loop your jewelry, ensure that you use round nose pliers to make the loop and then hold the bead steady by wrapping the wire around the loop.

Cutting wire

At some point, when working using wire, you will probably need to cut or trip your wire. You must clip the wire appropriately so that you avoid getting prodded, poked, or worse cut and scrapped. Using the wire cutters, you will end up with a side that is flat and a sharper or pointed side.

When cutting your jewelry, make sure the side that is flat is facing whichever piece that you are going to be using to work. This way, you will be able to cut the side until nicely flat so that it doesn't wind up sharp. You should hold either side while cutting to prevent the design you are holding from going flying.

Spiral

When it comes to wire wrapping, this particular style might be the hardest to master. Although this design may seem convoluted, with practice, you can learn them with ease. When forming a spiral, you need to create a loop using your pair of round nose pliers as you virtally would.

After completing your loop, take the flat nose pliers and place the loop in between the tips of the pliers, leaving the tip of your loop to stick out, then start to wrap the wire slowly with your fingers.

To avoid scratching the wire, ensure that your grip on the pliers is not too tight. Also, instead of trying to spiral a lengthy piece at once, adopt that are small and have constant rotation.

Enjoy yourself

Lastly, regardless of how many DIY jewelry pieces you make or how much you practice, just make sure you are having fun while doing it. Don't stress too much about obtaining the most neat cut wire or the perfect spiral. With practice, making exquisite pieces of jewelry will become more intuitive.

Chapter 5: How to Create Basic Wire Links

To create basic wire links, you need to:

Choose a medium-gauge wire

You will require a wire with enough thickness to be relatively sturdy since the links are load-bearing elements. Typically, half-hard wire with a 20 gauge is a suitable choice. Use of half-hard wire in place of dead soft may also aid in strengthening your links.

If you want to include beads in your jewelry, ensure that the wire you use is plently thin that it can penetrate the drill holes. You may require a higher gauge for beads that are very tiny.

Using the flush side of your cutters, cut off the extreme end of your wire. to make a flat edge, snip off a tiny bit of wire from the end of the wire that you are operating with.

The flush (flat) side of the wire clippers are supposed to be facing the length of wire you will be operating with (instead of the end that you are clipping off). That flat end of the wire is the one that you will use to make your loop.

Bead Jewelry

If you prefer, you can create your loop with the wire still attached to the roll; another option is to clip off a longer length of wire —30 cm (12 inches) or so— and then work with that. If you decide to cut off a piece the roll, do not make it very short, otherwise in the end you might not have enough wire to create your link.

If you intend to create a loop at the extreme end of a prefabricated finding like a headpin, you probably won't have to cut any of the wire off.

Using your round-nosed pliers, grasp the end of your wire. Clutch the extreme end of your wire gently in between the pliers. You need the wire to be flush the pliers so that you can hide the end stretching past the pliers when you check them in profile.

Since the pliers with the round-nose have ends that are tapered, you will need to place the end of the wire a bit near the base to make a larger loop and closer to the tip to create a loop that is tight.

Ensure you are careful enough not to press on the wire too much, otherwise you might end up denting it. You simply have to apply enough pressure to keep your wire in position.

To create a loop, gently roll the tip of the wire away from you. Turn the hand in hold of the pliers away from you once you

Bead Jewelry

have the wire in place securely, so that you have the wire beginning to wrap around one of the tips of the pliers. As you do this, use the thumb of the hand that is free to squeeze the wire against the pliers. Once you have twisted your wrist the furthest that it can go, reposition your pliers inside the loop so that you can begin turning them again.

Repeat this process until you achieve a finished loop. To ensure the loop does not come out a little misshapen, ensure that when repositioning the pliers, you leave the wire about the same length from the base of the pliers just as it had been when you began.

To center the loop, use the round nose pliers to rock the loop back. You should have a "p" shape once you complete wrapping the wire around the tips of your pliers. Place one of the pliers' jaws inside the loop then to position the loop centrally over the end of the wire, pinch the wire gently exactly at the base of the loop.

Using your free hand, grasp the wire tightly at the base of the loop, then using your pliers slightly bend back the wire so that you have the loop centrally positioned over the wire's length — similar to the dot of the letter "i." You might require the use of a chain nose pliers in place of the round nose pliers if the wire is very thick to mold into place

Bead Jewelry

Close the loop using the chain-nose pliers. After you are done with the loop, a small gap might be formed between the rest of your wire and the end of the loop. Work the end of the loop back and forth gently using your chain nose pliers while pushing it in until you close the gap. Be careful not to exert a lot of pressure on the sides of your loop from the outside; otherwise, you are going to yield a squashed loop.

For additional security, create a wrapped loop. Create a 90-degree bend in the wire about 5.1 cm (2 inches) using your chain nose pliers for an entirely closed loop with a slightly fancier appearance. Form a loop just above the bend as you usually would, but this time leave a "tail" that will extend before the wire at a right angle. Tightly wrap the tail around the wire beneath the bend for 3 to 4 times.

Using your cutters, clip off any remaining tail once done. If you want to, you may make the wrap more snug by squeezing it gently at the bottom and top using your fingernails or chain-nose pliers.

Once you get one bead on the wire, this technique is the easiest. When you create your right angle bend, grip the wire just above the bead —doing this is going to leave out a bit of space between the loop around which the tail will be wrapped and the bead.

Bead Jewelry

Once this loop is complete, you won't be able to open it. That means an element that you can open (such as a jump ring or a simple loop) must be attached to it.

If you like, you can add one or as much beads as you want on the wire. You can create a 2nd loop on the other side by sliding a bead onto the wire. Thus, you can attach a couple of beads together. You can also try dropping a bead onto a headpin that is flat-ended and create a loop on top of the bead. Then you could join the bead to an ear hook or a chain as a bangle or charm.

Chapter 6: How to Make Simple Wire-Wrapped Pendants

To make wire-wrapped pendants, you need to:

Choose a stone or another object for wrapping

In this particular project, you will be creating a cage or basket around the item with a cord to form a pendant that may be dangled on a necklace. You may use almost anything —you can use a crystal, tumbled stone, a coin, a piece of sea glass, or even a shark tooth or shell.

- When using this method, it's easiest to wrap items that are widest at the center and are irregularly shaped.

- Most pendants that are wrapped aren't more than approximately 5.1 centimeters (2") longer, but you have the freedom for wrapping larger objects. Remember that objects that are larger require more wire than the ones that are smaller.

Cut two medium-gauge wires of equal lengths

Select a wire for jewelry which is half hard and between 20 to 22 gauge. As the wire is required to carry the pendant's weight, using a fairly stronger wire is better. The required length depends on your pendant's size, but typically 15 to 20 cm (6–8 inches) is enough.

- Trim your wires using a wire clipper's flush side to ensure you get short, smart cuts.

- If testing out wire wrapping, it is best that you work with copper or any other base metal instead of a more high-priced treasured metal wire.

- Start using wire that is thicker such as eighteen gauge rather than twenty so that the wire can comfortably support its weight for heavier pendants.

Rotate the two wires together five times, beginning at the center

Use your two wires to create an "X," making sure both wires converge in the center. With the thumb and index finger, squeeze your wires at their point of intersection and perform five, strong twists, twisting the hands in converse directions.

- Make sure you properly twist both the wires and not just loop a wire around another.

On either side of your twist, yank your wires straight

When you finish twisting, you should have formed the shape of an X that has a twist at the centre. Take the tails of your wire then yank them straight and equally distant at an angle of approximately 90 degrees from your twist to form an "H."

- Pull your wires in between the fingers in your preferred direction to straighten them.

- You will repeat this process many times when making a pendant.

Place the twisted part on 1 side of the pendant

Select the side you want to position your pendant be it the back or front and position the twisted section of your wire against it flat. Your twist must be straight and strategically placed midway between the pendant's bottom and top.

- After having the twist firmly positioned, press down the wires along the pendant's surface, making sure to follow the outline of your pendant to the converse side.

Do the pendulum twist on the 2 wires at the bottom of the pendant

Take the 2 lower wires and make a second twist from the first one on the opposite side of the pendant. Make 5 twists, straighten the wires and force up the new twist so that it's laying flat against the pendant.

- The new twist will sit roughly across from the first. Now you should have a ring where the pendant's bottom can rest safely.

Carry on making twists until you get to the pendulum top

Take one of the cables on top of the first 2 twists, and create a new twist. As you did before, layer it against the pendant flat.

Continue with this process on both sides until you cover the whole pendant, up to the top.

- Now the pendant appears be trapped in a "cage" wire with 4 dangling wires over the top.

- Modify the cage as you proceed, so that it blends efficiently with your pendant. This can be done by pressing the stone flush occasionally against the twists you've already created, and yanking your wires taut.

Twist 2 of the wires together on top of the cage

Choose one of the other pairs of wires and twist it 5 times but without positioning the pendant and the wires flat against each other this time. Let them stick straight up, instead.

- That is the first stage in making the brace since that's the ring that you'll use to mount your pendant.

Tie every remaining 2 wires around the final twist

Wind the 2 free wires 5 times one after the other around the twist that is vertical or at least until you hit the twist top. Once done, use your wire cutters to clip off the ends.

- Slowly and carefully twist these wires to create a coil that is strong and tight. For leverage, you may utilize the chain nose pliers here if you wish.

- Before snipping them off, it might be beneficial if you used your pliers to draw the stray ends of the wire tauts. After snipping the wires, pinch off any ends which stick out using your pliers.

Turn the 2 top wires to form a loop around a pencil

Flatten the wires above the knot. Ensure that they form a "T" shape at a right angle with the twist. Position a pencil above the twist and tie your 2 wires in opposing directions to form a nice round loop. You can also use any item that has a round cross-section —such as the jaw of a pair of round-nose pliers.

Verify that the the 2 wires have been wrapped tightly on your loop and near each other.

Turn the rest of the wire around the twist to have the bail secured

If your bail is pleasing, grab the ends of the both wires then loop them around the twist twice or thrice. Make sure your wraps are tidy and tight. When done, remove the pencil; you need to have a bail that is comfortable (secure) for your pendant.

- Clip off the tips of the cords, once done then straighten them using the chain-nose pliers.

- To achieve a classier feel, use the tip of your round-nose pliers to create a tiny loop at the end of every cable. Coil each wire in a spiral using the chain-nose pliers then straighten the spirals on each side against the bottom part of the twist.

Chapter 7: How to Make a Basic 2-Wire Weave

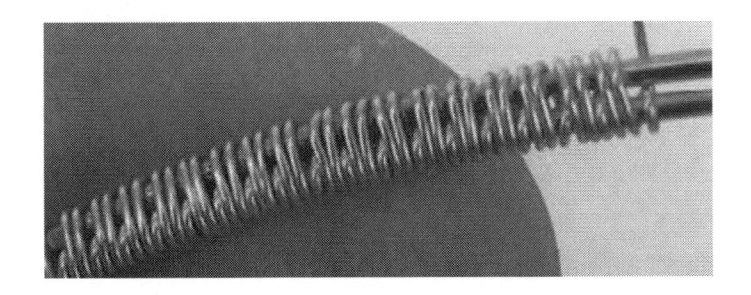

To make a basic 2-wire weave, you need to:

Choose a few medium wire and fine wire (gauge: 16 to 20) and (gauge: 24 to 26) respectively

The wire that is thicker forms your weave's backbone, and then you twist the wire that is thinner around it. Ideally, the wire that is thicker should be semi-hard; wire that is dead soft is most suitable for the elements that are woven.

- Because getting acquainted with wire weaving requires some practice, you might want to begin with copper or any other comparatively cheap wire.

Cut 2 medium wire bits to the preferred length

The required length is going to depend on your design. For instance, if you are creating a simple woven ring, a good length is about 8.9 cm (3.5 inches).

- If you so desire, while it's on the roll still, you may use the wire for fine weaving. If not, snip off a length that's not less than 30 cm (12 inches) so that you'll have plenty with which to work.

On your work surface, position the two warp wires each parallel to the other

Based on the look you want to achieve, you can place them as near or as far away from each other as you want. Please note that the farther apart your warp wires are, the more you'll use extra weaving wire to account for whichever size.

- You can collect the tips of the warp wires then hold them in place on the same side as the masking tape. You can also try securing them in place using a ring clamp or pinch them in between your fingertips.

- The wires do not need to be precisely parallel. When you position the two warp wires a bit apart or when you tilt at least one of them, it can create an interesting effect that causes the weave to be extensive in some areas than in others.

Twist the wire for weaving around the underside of the warp wire once

Beginning near the tip of the weaving thread, place the wire against the bottom warp's front and loop it once around, away from you. Make sure you tie the wire at the bottom wire. To ensure you make a solid coil, hold the wire taut.

- The wire for weaving must run through the warp wire's front when the coil is complete.

- Do not commence weaving the wire at the tip. You could try leaving out some of the tail around 2.5–5.1 cm (1–2 inches) so that once done you can hold down the weave.

- You may want to begin the weaving not less than 1.9 cm (0.75 inches) from the tips of your warp wires based on what you intend to do with your woven wire.

Place the wire for weaving below the warp wire at the top then tie it twice

Pull the weaving wire to go past the warp wire at the top and loop it twice around the wire on top. At this instance, instead of drawing the wire away from you, pull it towards you. Your wire for weaving will wind up on the front of the warp wire on top.

- In case the resulting coils aren't tight enough together, you may use your fingernails to jolt them below your warp wires. Avoid using pliers since it can damage your wire.

Position the wire for weaving behind the warp wire at the bottom and coil two times

Twist the wire for weaving away from yourself. you must begin the design over from here and proceed until the weave gains the intended length.

- When you create more coils between every loop, you can change the pattern. For example, you can alternate between doing two coils on one side then four on the other.

- While you become more familiar with weaving methods that entail the use of two wires, start by testing out weaves that integrate three warp wires or more.

Clip off the tips of your warp wire and squish them in

After you have your desired length, snip off your warp wire tails using some wire clippers. Tenderly squeeze in any edges that are sharp using the chain nose pliers.

- For more stability, you may add a few additional coils on either end.

Assimilate the wire that has been woven into a bracelet, ring, pendant or necklace

Woven wire may offer many forms of jewelry an impressive addition. When you have the wire threaded, you can use pliers or your hands to fold it into your preffered shape.

- When making a simple and proper ring, for instance, wrap a small section approximately 8.9 cm (3.5") of woven wire round a ring axis. Fold the four tips of your warp wires into graceful spirals using the round-nosed pliers.

- You may also make stunning pendants that integrate undrilled stones or beads using woven wire.

Bead Jewelry

Chapter 8: Sword Pendant Wire Wrapped Jewelry

To make this Sword pendant, you need:

Supplies

All the wire used in this project is round copper that is dead soft. This wire can be acquired at your local hardware store; alternatively, you can use copper wire that is stripped or simply use scrap. The gauges are adjustable, but ensure that the wire you use for your base is not less than 18g.

1 or more 2 to 6mm gemstone bead(s)

3 inch 24g wire for attaching beads

Bead Jewelry

12 inch of 21g wire for ornamentation

10 inch of 18g wire for the base

One jump ring

Wire Cutter

Round Nose Pliers

Flat Nose Pliers

Clear nail polish

Emery board

Metal block to hammer

Ruler

Hammer

Patina (optional)

Sealer (optional)

Directions

The completed sword is going to be approximately two inches, but if you prefer a distinct size you can recalibrate the wire lengths.

Step 1: Start

Begin by cutting one copper wire (gauge: 18) strand to be around ten inches in length. At around 6 inches, bend the wire.

Step 2: create a point

Squeeze the tip using your flat-nose pliers until its very tight. Twist one wire at a right angle at around two inches from the point. Do the same with the back side.

Step 3: Beginning the Cross-Guard (handle)

Bend one wire at a right angle using the thickest part of the flat nose pliers for length reference. Repeat this step using your other wire.

Step 4: Cross-Guard

Take one of the wires and fully bend it, then make it as tight as the point at the bottom. Do the same with the remaining wire.

Bend either wire at a right angle in order to have the ends pointing towards the top aligned with the base of your sword.

Step 5: Mold the Cross-guard

Depending on the sword style you want, bend your cross-guard downwards or upwards using the flat-nose pliers. Curve the cross-guard a tiny bit.

Step 6: Work the blade

Using a chasing hammer and a block of metal —you can also use whatever you got —hammer all sides of the sword gently to flatten it out. The sword will get wider as you continue to hammer.

As you hammer, try to ensure that the thickness is even throughout. Keep hammering until the sword flattens out and has a shape and thickness you desire. If preferred, you may also make the cross-guard flat.

Step 7: shape the sword's tip

Hammer the tip of your sword gently until a point forms. To make the shape more precise, smooth the rounded tip of your sword using an emery board until you form the pointed tip. Don't let it get too sharp.

Fun fact

For soft metals such as copper, emery boards are considered to be very suitable for filing them.

Step 8: Make the grip and pommel

Using your flat-nose pliers, bend the tail of one of the wire's end at 90 degrees, about .75 inches above the cross guard.

Step 9: Pommel loop

Using your round nose pliers, grasp the tail of the wire where it bends. Then, using your fingers, loop the tail of the wire over the pliers and form into a circular shape.

Step 10: create the grip

In the space left above the cross guard, twist the remaining tail of the wire around the other wires; this is going to yield not less than 5 or 6 full wraps. If the wire is long enough, you can continue wrapping until you are satisfied after that, and you can work your way above the cross-guard. To add stability, use pliers on the grip. If you wish, you can also cut the excess wire.

Step 11: Patina

At this stage, you incorporate the patina into the swords. These are near done, and if you don't care for extra aesthetics, you can finish them now.

Pro tip

If you desire to have the ability to make areas that will be partialy hidden later to look outstanding, incorporate the patina in stages.

Step 14: Rinse

Rinse off the chemicals from your sword once dark enough, then pat dry

Step 15: Buff

Using hand buffing sheets, a Dremel, or another rotary buffer, begin scraping off the heavy patina. Polish until every low point is black, and the high points are shiny.

Pro tip

If you want, you may leave out some parts (such as the cross-guard or grip) all black.

At this point, you can simply incorporate a jump ring then decide that your are done and the sword is complete — or you can just keep going.

Step 16: Add gems

To attach gem(s), cut 3 inches of a 24g wire. If your beads are translucent, brush the middle of the wire with clear nail polish and let the polish dry before you start working with it.

Pro tip

When operating with patina and translucent beads, brush the wire with the clear nail polish before you add the beads.

Step 17: Choose beads

Select your preferred beads then incorporate them to the 3-inch wire. Test out how the beads feel around the cross-guard or grip.

Step 18: Incorporate the gems

After you find a way of designing the beads that you like, firmly attach the beads by winding the tips of the thin wire round the cross guard. For additional security, have the wire wrapped around the beads as well.

Step 19: Decorative points

For ornamentation, cut out a 12-inch scrap of wire that is 21g. You can use what you have since this length is alterable. Curve the wire into half, then pinch the end into a tight tip using a pair of flat-nose pliers. Measure around an inch from the ending tip then curve one of the wires at a right angle.

Step 20: Incorporating the ornaments

Curve the other wire in the opposite direction at a right angle. Line up the decorative point in the middle of the blade.

Wrap all the tips around one of the handles of the cross-guard, which will give you about 4-inches of wire to use as ornamentation on either side. That is now the part where you need to be creative – make up a design you like. Start twisting the wires around the grip, cross-guard and the gems.

Have a jump ring attached to a pommel or backs and fronts of swords

Step 21: Patina

Spread a patina layer onto the newly made wire ornamentation.

Step 22: Antique

Start taking off the heavy patina using hand buffing sheets or Dremel or another rotary buffer. Buff until each of the low points are black, and the high points are shiny.

Step 23: Finishing

You have completed the sword. Apply a jewelry grade sealer for protecting the finish if desired. Attach a chain then wear.

Chapter 9: Wrapped Stacked Wire Ring

This pattern looks difficult to make, but, in reality, it's not. The trick is creating a bunch of rings from your wire, then stacking and binding all of them at the base. Sounds easy, doesn't it?

Supplies

5 wire scraps for the stacks of simple rings: The wire you use should be round and soft in gauges of 20, 18 or 16. This pattern uses copper wire with 18 gauge

The length of all scraps of wire are supposed have the same circumference as that of the knuckle at the middle of the finger that will be wearing the ring, and an additional three centimeters. For instance, if the finger intended for the ring measures 5.5cm, add 3 more centimeters to get a wire that is 8.5cm long.

1 scrap of soft wire that is round and has a length of 9 cm in 20 or 18 gauge —used for joining the stacked rings together; this pattern uses copper wire with 20 gauge.

Chain nose pliers

Round nose pliers

Flat nose pliers

Wirecutter

Ring mandrel (or another cylinder that is sturdy and is about your finger's circumference)

Nylon or Plastic hammer for jewelry to shape the ring around your mandrel

Optional

A single bead that will act as the focal point on the ring

The green bead used in this pattern is six mm round Czech glass

1 scrap of soft round 16, 18, or 20 gauge wire fifteen centimeters in length, to create an extra stacking ring which

is going to add the bead to the major ring. This pattern uses copper wire with 20 gauge

*Ensure that this wire can easily run through the opening in the bead you will be attaching.

Directions

Begin by creating 5 simple rings which are going to be stacked to form the major ring.

Cut out the 5 pieces of wire; ensure that each wire is the same circumference as the middle knuckle of the finger intended for the ring and an additional 3 cm. The wires used in this pattern measures 8.5 centimeters to make a completed ring of size 7.

Take one of the wires and create a tiny loop on one tip of your wire using the ends of your round nose pliers.

Straighten the loop and flatten it using your flat nose pliers.

At the tip of the wire, create a loop; make sure the loop faces away from your initial loop.

Take one wire that is loop ended that you just created then place on the ring mandrel.

*Occasionally, the wire "springs back" a bit after you have wrapped the wire around your mandrel, thus making your

ring a bigger size. It, therefore, might be a good idea to use a size smaller on your mandrel than you like your completed ring to be.

For instance, in this case, the finished ring is going to be size seven, as mentioned, so on the mandrel we'll place the wire on size six.

With a tiny space between the ends of the wire loop, wrap either side of the wire all round the mandrel.

nicely Pound the ends that are looped around the curve of the mandrel using your nylon or plastic hammer.

To ensure that it's a good fit, slide down the ring on your mandrel to your preferred completed size. Repeat this procedure with the other 4 wires. You should now have a pile of 5 simple rings.

Optional

Incorporate a bead on your ring. We will be making an extra simple ring with the bead mounted on if you wish to include a bead in the finished ring.

To make sure that your bead is at the central point of your wire, slide your fifteen centimeter long wire through the bead.

Next, fold down the ends of your wire towards the base of the bead. Your wires need to be crossing one another at the base of the bead.

Proceed to fold the scraps around the base of the bead until the wires are laying across the bead's underside flat.

Next, use the mandrel to shape your wires into rings. In this case, since our finished ring size will be 7 the size of the ring on your mandrel will be 6.

Firmly twist the wires all round your mandrel, making sure that the base of the bead is pressed up on the mandrel until the tips of the wire point upwards on both sides of your bead.

Slip the ring of the bead below the mandrel until you get to your selected completed size.

Next twist the wire points of the bead ring into spirals or loops using the ends of your round nose pliers.

What's left is to collect together all the simple rings to make the stacked ring that is wrapped.

Stack together the simple rings in whichever order you prefer. If you had created a simple ring having one bead attached to it, you should place it in the center of your stack.

Position the loops on the sides and top to create a nice pattern after sliding the rings.

If the shanks and loops overlap one another in some areas, it is perfectly fine – this just adds interest and depth to your design.

Bind together the stacks of rings at the base using the nine centimeter wire scrap.

Squeeze down the wrap firmly into place using your flat nose pliers after each wrap of the wire for binding. Trim the binding wire's ends after wrapping the binding wire a couple of times on the base of the stack of rings so that they will wind up on the ring shank's interior.

Tightly squeeze the tips of your binding wire that are trimmed against the shank of the ring using the flat nose pliers so that they will not scrattle you as you put on your finished ring.

You are now done making the ring.

Bead Jewelry

Chapter 10: Old Fashioned Chain Wire

To make this piece of jewelry

Supplies

1 clasp of your choice

Half hard wire round or square – 1 1/16 inch straight wire per link – 3 links per inch finished chain.

You can use nearly any wire gauge; just remember that the bigger the gauge is, the harder it's going to be to form the links, and it also increases the chances of your fingers "falling off."

Tools needed

Permanent marker (Sharpie)

Flush wire cutters

Chain nose pliers

Round nose pliers

Ruler

Cleaning cloth

Directions

Step 1:

Sort your wire by gauge 18 – 20 – 21. Cut your scrap to length then start making a chain. If you want a chain or you don't have a lot of scrap lying around, cut out your wires to be 1 1/16 inches long.

Step 2:

Create a mark on your round nose plies that is roughly 5 to 7 mm from the tip using a permanent marker. Most people opt for smaller loops —make sure it's not very tiny.

Step 3:

The secret to perfecting this craft is in how you hold the pliers. It may seem a bit awkward at first, but with time it definitely will get easier. You begin each twist with the palm side up. Otherwise, you will feel and look as if you are attempting an impossible yoga position by the time you finish the turn if you begin with your palm facing down.

Use the index finger of your free hand to hold the chain that you are working on and the dominant hand to hold the pliers

Step 4:

Without forgetting to palm up, clasp the wire roughly 5/16 inches from the tip of the wire using your pliers then holding it against your index finger.

Step 5:

Folding the wire, turn over your hand until the wire's tip comes into contact with your finger at the top of the wire.

Step 6:

To ensure that the loop you just created is at the top, turn the link around, and then using your pliers, grasp the tip of the wire that is free once again at 5/16 inches from the wire's tip. Remember to palm up.

Step 7:

Turn over your hand again —as you did in step 5. When the tip of the wire comes into contact with your finger inside the initial loop, stop right away this time. You just finished your first link.

To form a fair amount of links, you will now need to do over steps 4 to 7 to create a significant number of links (otherwise, your finger my fall off).

*Keep in mind that approximately 3 links will form 1 inch of chain.

Step 8:

You can make sure that you get a beautiful chain by making sure each of the links are facing a similar direction. With the initial loop facing the exact position that you made it – upwards- open one link.

Step 9:

Onto the opened loop, slide in a closed link.

Step 10:

Seal off the first link

Step 11:

Open up the link you have just attached

Step 12:

Proceed to do over steps 8 through 11 until you achieve your preferred length of chain.

Step 13:

Attach a clasp of your choosing —be it a handmade one or a standard one— and you are all set.

This design of jewelry will also look just as good in either square or round wire. To create your version of a Figaro chain, you may even include wire links that are twisted to your straight links.

Bead Jewelry

Chapter 11: Turtle Bracelet

*Each turtle link will be about 1¼ to 1½ inches long

Materials (for each turtle link)

1, 12mm Flat Oval Bead

1, 24" 24-gauge round dead soft wire

1, 8" 21-gauge round dead soft wire

Tools

Round nose pliers

Flat nose pliers

Chain nose pliers

Ruler

Wire cutters

Directions

Straighten and cut one piece of 21 gauge round silver wire for each turtle link. Sculpt the shape of a spiny turtle body beginning ¾ inches from one end. The tip of the head to the beginning of the rear leg should measure about 1 inch.

Tape together both of the wire ends. Gently shape the bottom wire of the read legs towards the tail using round nose pliers.

Leaving a ¾" end and using the 24 gauge copper wire from the spool or coil, wrap the copper wire near the tail around the base of one leg then wrap around the tail twice. Slide on a bead and then proceed to center it over the body.

Wrapping twice around, attach the wire that is beaded to the neck. Don't cut the copper wrap wire that is 24 gauge. Go back and take the ¾ inch you had left at the beginning end to make a coil.

Work around each of the turtle's appendages, still using the copper wire that is 24 gauge, wrapping in rotation around the turtle's body until the wire is almost gone. Wrapping the wire around the neck twice, end the wrap wire at the neck then tuck it under the frame wire beneath the bead.

Bead Jewelry

Bend the turtle's legs into natural poses using a pair of flat, chain, and round nose pliers as well as your fingers. Cut the silver frame wire (21 gauge) to ensure the ends are ½" long. Create a hook using a round nose pliers and as you do that, make sure you work with both wires as if you are working with just one. Head towards the back, then insert the hook right through another turtle's head, making sure you close it firmly.

Repeat steps 1 through 4 to make as many turtle links as you want then link them together to form a bracelet. You may add either a lobster claw clasp or a trigger to close the bracelet or make your one such as the double wrapped hook

Chapter 12: Figure 8 Chain

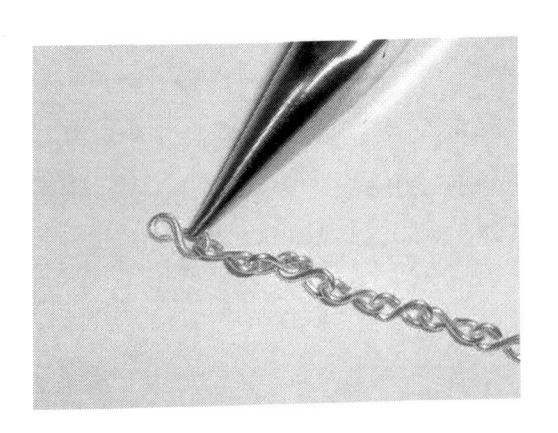

This project is an ideal way to use little scraps of 18 and 20 gauge wire. You can use square, round or half round wire or a mixture to form a pattern in your chain. Since the links are solid, you can use them on their own as an alternative to jump rings; you can also connect them to form a chain.

Materials

18 Gauge Round Half Hard 1/10 Sterling Silver Filled Wire

20 Gauge Round Half Hard 1/10 Sterling Silver Filled Wire

Tools

Premium Nylon Jaw Pliers

5 inch Plato Slim Flush Cutters for Wire Working or Beading

Round Nose Wire Plier

Chain Nose Wire Plier

Directions

***NOTE:**

3 inches of wire yields approximately 1 inch of chain; thus, 50ft of wire is going to yield a chain of roughly 20 inches. For this pattern, you can use any 18g or 20g wire. However, craft wires can be a bit too soft to hold securely. 18g is always stronger. The wires recommended for this pattern is half hard silver filled. You can also use sterling wire as an alternative.

Step 1:

If you are using scrap wire, the first thing you need to do to make the chain or connectors is to sort and size your pieces of wire. For the 18 gauge wire, you will need pieces that are ¾" long; for the 20 gauge, they need to be 2/3" long. This pattern is going to work with the 20 gauge wire.

Ensure your pieces of wire are straight. If your wires need straightening, do so by holding one end with the chain nose pliers, then pull through the jaws of the nylon pliers.

Step 2:

For the chain to be an even size, you must make each link identical. The easiest way to do this is by marking your round nose pliers so that you form each loop at the same point. We, however, need to find this point first.

Check the middle of your wire then mark it using your marker pen. That should be the point where the two ends of the wire meet. You need to do this on the first piece of wire only.

Step 3:

Using your round nose pliers, grasp the piece of wire at the very end – close to their tip— and then create a loop. Make sure that the end and the point you had marked on the wire meet at the central point. To do this, hold the other end of the wire between your fingers then turn the pliers to form a loop.

Step 4:

For the end of the wire to line up with your pen mark perfectly, you might need to attempt step 2 a couple of times to find the perfect point on your pliers. Once you have identified this point, use your marker pen to mark the pliers, and then just make sure you make each future loop around this point.

Step 5:

Using your chain nose pliers, grasp the first loop so that you have the straight piece of wire pointing downwards towards your hand. Form a second loop in the opposite direction of the first. You can do this by grasping the straight end of the wire using the round nose pliers at the point where you had made the pen mark on the jaw. Make sure that the end of the wire is in line with the pen mark.

Step 6:

Grasp the wire shape with the chain nose pliers carefully so that one jaw is against the opposite side of the same loop, and the other is against the end of the wire and squeeze gently. Repeat with the other side. Each end should now be sitting against the central wire, forming a straight line, making a complete figure 8 shape.

Step 7:

To ensure the ends don't stick out at all so that they don't catch anything, and that the shape is entirely flat, squeeze both sides between the jaws of the chain nose tightly. Doing this also helps harden the wire.

Step 8:

Once you've made a few, you can start to connect the links to form a chain. Twist one end upwards using the chain nose pliers to open one loop. To avoid weakening the wire, do not pull open.

Step 9:

Take another figure 8 shape and thread the closed loop onto the loop you just opened in step 8. To ensure you don't have any snaggy ends, twist the closed loop using your chain nose pliers then squeeze between the jaws.

You can speed up production by working in batches. Take various lengths of wire and form the first loop, then create the second loop and close all loops and so on. This way, you will be able to complete the chain much faster.

Step 10:

Continue adding figures of 8 connectors until your chain achieves your desired length. Add connectors the same way, attach a clasp, then thread on your favorite pendant to complete the design.

Bead Jewelry

Chapter 13: Grape Cluster Earrings

Supplies

Leaf beads of some form. This pattern uses big and glass

Pearls —or other beads— in your preferred grape color; you can get freshwater pearls that exist in different varieties that are dyed —and are cheap

Jump rings. These are little wire bits that are circular, and with a break in them

Earring hooks

Headpins; these are bits of wire that are straight having a bit that is flat at the end to prevent your beads from slipping off. If you don't have access to this, you can create one with wire by twisting a very small loop at the tip.

You can get the above supplies from many of the chain craft stores around the country. You could also check them from local bead stores.

Tools

Round-nose pliers. Having 2 pairs of pliers (where one is for holding and the other for bending) might help, although many commercial headpins are malleable enough to curve by pinching using your fingers.

Wire cutters

Directions

Attach a pearl to a headpin

About at the center of your round nose pliers, grasp the wire above the bead. Mark or simply take note of where you grip the wire – so that your wire is of equal distance on every piece when you bend it; you need to grab every other "grape" in the exact spot.

Curve your wire at a right angle

You now need to adjust your hold on your wire. You will want the pliers to be on the flip side of the right angle as they had been initially, and once more, you will want to be keen on where you are grabbing the wire and attempt to pelt that

Bead Jewelry

exact place on the pliers each time. Doing this makes each of the completed grapes look uniform, which is something nice to aspire for, but not something you need to obsess over.

Create a loop by twisting the wire over the pliers

Halfway through, you will need to adjust your grasp once more so that you can cross the tip of your wire around itself at the base of your loop. When you complete your piece, the stem of the "grape" and the free end of the wire needs to again remain at a right angle.

Going slowly and keeping your wraps tight, twist the tip of the wire that is free across the stem (having the free end at a right angle is what causes the wraps to look presentable) until it reaches over the top of the bead. At this step, on your wire having a lengthy tail is going to help. To simplify management, you can try buying headpins that are extra-long.

Clip

Clip off the rest of the tail from your wire as nearly possible to the bead. You should not leave out a tiny bit because you can poke yourself with it. If you can not get as near as you need bend in any bits that are pointy nearer to the stem using your pliers.

You have now completed your first grape. You now need to create 19 more so that you have 20 in total. Each earring requires ten grapes.

Open up a jump ring

As a jewelry newbie, note that you should clasp the ring at both sides of the break, then curve the tips PAST each other. You don't want to distort the loop by gripping either side, then pulling them apart – your ring should remain as round as it can so that you can change it back again.

Slide a single bead on the jump ring and grip either side of the gap and bring the tips back together to bend it closed again.

Open up a separate jump ring, then string along the first jump ring/bead combination and another bead onto the second ring before you close it. You now have a chain of 2 jump rings with several beads attached – since you will be adding more jump rings onto the chain, make sure you keep a close eye on the "top" ring.

Continue adding more jump rings/beads in a sequence of bead-jump ring -bead. You can ensure the earrings don't get lopsided by ensuring that each jump ring has 2 beads with the chain centered until you have used upto 10 beads.

Work on the lead bead

It's now time to handle the leaf bead. The bead we used for this pattern has an opening through the top, which means that it is going to be linked using a single jump ring through the so-called hole.

You may get some beads that have the holes running through the leaf from top to bottom. In this case, you have to string them on a headpin like the rest of the grapes.

No matter which type of leaf bead you got, just affix it to the ring at the top of your grape cluster. Link in the earring hook next. Some earring hooks can close and open the way a jump ring does, while others will require to be attached to/with a jump ring, and you will now have a single grape cluster earring. Make the other pair using the same process.

Step 14: Fabric Wrapped Necklace Choker

To make this necklace:

Materials and supplies

Artistic wire (or another wire) to secure the edges of the fabric to your wireframes by wrapping them.

You will require not less than 4 pieces each measuring 12.7 centimeters (5 inches) long

If your strips of fabric are less than sixty inches long, you will require more than four scraps of wire. This pattern uses a 20 gauge Artistic wire that is gunmetal colored.

2 strips soft fabric that is not startchy

Bead Jewelry

This pattern uses an Ultrasuede that includes a metallic print that is floral and a jersey knit camouflage print that measure about 152.4 centimeters (60 inches) long and 3.81 centimeters (1.5 inches) wide each. You may use several strips that are shorter to build up the two strips 60 inches in length if your fabric isn't 60 inches long.

16-gauge round soft wire – this pattern uses brass — 167.64 cm (66") of wire

2 jump rings –fifteen mm in size (this pattern uses antique brass).

Tape measure.

Wirecutter

A file, cup burr, or knife sharpening stone for smoothing off the 16-gauge wire ends.

Flat nose pliers

Round nose pliers

Scissors for cutting your fabric

Optional:

Clasp (an S-shape or a hook suits this design well). This pattern ever used a clasp, and it worked out just fine.

Directions

The first thing you need to do is measure the neck of the person the choker is intended for using a tape measure then set the tape up to your preferred length of the choker.

Add 3.81 centimeters (1.5 inches) to the length you got so that you can now have the total length you will be using.

In that total length you will require four pieces of the sixteen gauge wire. For instance, for a 16 inch long choker, you will require four wire pieces measuring 16" + 1.5"=17.5" long (70" of wire in total) each

For the choker:

Cut the four scraps of sixteen gauge wire

Do not flatten out the wire; allow it to retain its original curve

Smooth and round off either points of all pieces of the 16 gauge wires using your knife sharpening stone, cup burr, or file.

Form a circular shape from every piece of the sixteen gauge wire using only your hands.

You can also try shaping the wires into circles by wrapping them around a huge box of oatmeal or another large cylinder.

Bead Jewelry

Create loops on every tip of all the sixteen gauge wires using the thickest part of your round nose pliers.

Cut out your 3.81 centimeters (1.5 inches) x 152.4 cetimeters (60 inches) piece from each of your fabrics; you can also try cutting a couple of strips that are smaller to add up to the 60-inch length out of every fabric

Cut out the four scraps from your Artistic wire to measure 12.7 centimeters (5 inches) long each

If you would like to create wraps that are artistically messy, you may cut out longer pieces of wire. You will require more than four pieces of this wire if your strips of fabric are less than 60 inches so that you can create additional wraps at every place where you incorporate new strips into the wrap of fabric.

Take one of the sixteen gauge wires and begin to wrap one of the strips of fabric

Layer one of the Artistic wire —binding wires—against the start of the wrap of fabric, and then using your pliers (flat nose), pinch together the artistic wire and the sixteen gauge wire that is fabric-wrapped

Twist the long point of the artistic wire all round your fabric very tightly using the fingers of your free hand.

Bead Jewelry

To ensure the fabric does not later on get dettached with the sixteen gauge wire, make sure you have a good tight wire binding.

You can neatly wrap the binding wire or you can turn it to be artfully messy

Once you have wrapped the whole wire for binding around the 16 gauge wire tip that is fabric-wrapped, clamp down the 2 ends securely using your pliers.

Ensure that you have no scratchy ends of the binding wire sticking out

Using artistic wire bindings to secure either tips of your fabric wrap, twist another strip of fabric around the other sixteen gauge wire.

Twist all your jump rings using the flat nose pliers until they open up

Take one of the wires that are wrapped with fabric and place one jump ring on every end loop

Link the jump rings to every plain sixteen gauge wire one at a time, and then add the other wires that are wrapped fabric onto your jump rings

Twine your jump rings using the flat nose pliers until closed

The 2 metal wires that are bare will be sandwiched between the 2 wires that are fabric wrapped.

This pattern for the choker is pliable as the wires can be bent to perfectly fit the neck so that it is very simple to wear and remove

Recommendations for wearing the choker

Put on the choker to have the end that is open at the back – if you prefer, you can attach a clasp

With the use of a jump ring that is sufficiently huge to ran through all four wires, you may even include a pendant on your design, or you could just hang your pendant on only one wire

If you like, you can also put on the choker with the end that is open in the front then incorporate some kind of dangling ornaments onto your jump rings

Bead Jewelry

Chapter 15: DIY Anthropology Perched Harmonies Necklace

To make this:

Materials required

4 mm round glass beads –assorted colors

2 jump rings

Clasps for your necklace

A gold necklace chain

Thinner gold wire

Gold wire that is thick –this pattern uses craft wire that is 3mm in diameter; you can find this from a hardware store.

Pliers

You will also require a hammer and a surface that is hard enough to make the pendant. You can use a regular hammer from your garage, but it will give the wire a rustic texture. The best option is to use a jewelry-making hammer as it is going to give you a smooth shine. Another alternative is hammering using a stainless steel bench block, which is going to give your project a professional look.

Just as the Anthropology necklace uses gemstone beads that are faceted, this pattern uses plain 4mm glass rounds.

Directions

Step 1: form the wire pendant

Take your thick wire and snip off a bit less than 3 inches. You can work in the garage or any other nice hard surface. If you don't have the bench block, the sidewalk could work. While hammering down, grab the tip of one wire, and carefully flatten the wire gently as you work.

Do not hammer the wire super-flat; just slightly. Make sure that the pressure you use on the entire wire is even throughout. Hammer the tip additionally harder once it looks slightly flat to seemingly "press" the wire outwards, thus making it even flatter.

Step 2: Create the holes

Position a small ice pick with the pointy tip right at the end of your wire. You can improvise and use a screwdriver - or a nail that is tougher - if you don't posses an ice pick. You just require something having a tip that is somewhat fine. To make the holes, hammer this through either sides of your wire.

Step 3: Incorporate the beads on the pendant

Wrap the end of the thin gold wire (about 10 inches) several times around one tip of the wire that has been hammered until tightly secured, and then add the beads through the other point.

The sequence of placing the beads is very critical if you want to achieve a good look; the pattern for the necklace starts with clear yellow to yellow to opaque mint, to blue, to purple, to pink, to clear, to red, to orange, to jade, to pink, then red, and finally blue.

If you do not get the beads in the specified colors—some of the colors used for our pattern were a little bit distinct shades— or you just don't care about it looking exactly alike, you can go with whatever you want.

Begin to load the pendant with the beads. Place a bead exactly infront of your wire, and then yank tightly with your right hand as you hold the bead using your left hand.

Bring the wire that is thin below your pendant, then up behind the side at the back and back below over the front side. To attach the bead to the pendant securely, continue for around three more times before you add another bead. Proceed with every other bead until you have attached all twelve on.

With all your beads strung, you should have some excess wire remaining; wrap this until near the hole. Then, clip and fold the clipped tip over the back to conceal it.

Step 4: Attach the jump rings to the pendant

To either end, attach wires of equal lengths then to form the necklace, add the clasps to the ends of your wire that are loose. The Anthro necklace is seventeen inches long, but if you want, you may modify the length.

That's it! Your piece is complete!

Conclusion

Try different colors such as copper, bronze, silver, etc. if you want to experiment. Just ensure your metal color matches. You could also use different styles and colors of beads (wood, metal beads, plastic, crystals, whatever!) to match your personality.